BIOGRAPHY FROM
ANCIENT CIVILIZATIONS
LEGENDS, FOLKLORE, AND STORIES OF ANCIENT WORLDS

The Life and Times of

CATHERINE THE GREAT

Mitchell Lane
PUBLIS

P.O. Box 196
Hockessin, Delaware
www.mitchelllane.com

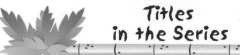

BIOGRAPHY FROM
ANCIENT CIVILIZATIONS
LEGENDS, FOLKLORE, AND STORIES OF ANCIENT WORLDS

Titles
in the Series

The Life and Times of:

BIOGRAPHY FROM
ANCIENT CIVILIZATIONS
LEGENDS, FOLKLORE, AND STORIES OF ANCIENT WORLDS

The Life and Times of

CATHERINE THE GREAT

Karen Bush Gibson

Printing   1   2   3   4   5   6   7   8

Library of Congress Cataloging-in-Publication Data

Gibson, Karen Bush.
    The life and times of Catherine the Great: by Karen Gibson.
        p. cm. — (Biography from ancient civilizations)
    Includes bibliographical references and index.
    ISBN 1-58415-347-4 (library bound)
    1. Catherine II, Empress of Russia, 1729-1796—Juvenile literature. 2. Russia—History—Catherine II, 1762-1796—Juvenile literature. 3. Empresses—Russia—Biography—Juvenile literature. I. Title. II. Series.
    DK170.G53 2005
    947'.063'092—dc22
                                                                                2005009685

ABOUT THE AUTHOR: Karen Bush Gibson has been a freelance writer for more than 16 years. She has had many articles published in such publications as *Boys' Life*, *Backpacker* and *Army Times*. She also teaches writing. With a special gift for telling a story, Ms. Gibson is the author of more than 20 educational books for children. She lives in Oklahoma with her husband and three sons.

PHOTO CREDITS: Cover, pp. 1, 3, 6 — Superstock; p. 12 — Andrea Pickens; p. 18 — Getty Images; pp. 21, 26 — Superstock; p. 31 — Andrea Pickens; p. 34 — Getty Images

PUBLISHER'S NOTE: This story is based on the author's extensive research, which she believes to be accurate. Documentation of such research is contained on page 47.

The internet sites referenced herein were active as of the publication date. Due to the fleeting nature of some web sites, we cannot guarantee they will all be active when you are reading this book.

The Life and Times of

CATHERINE THE GREAT

*For Your Information

One of Catherine the Great's favorite pastimes was riding horses. She spent much of her time alone as a child. Horses and books were her companions.

CHAPTER
ONE

THE ARRIVAL

Figchen took a deep breath as her sleigh came to a stop. She took the arm of an escort as she stepped to the ground. It had been a long trip, made even more difficult because the 14-year-old girl hadn't been allowed to ride her horse. Her mother stood before her, wrapped in furs to fight the icy chill in the air and tapping her foot impatiently.

This trip was very important to Figchen's mother. She had worked hard to get an invitation from Empress Elizabeth of Russia. Her mother believed that Figchen would be a good wife for Elizabeth's nephew, the 15-year-old Grand Duke Peter. So now it was time for Figchen to grow up. She had to give up her nickname and become known by her real name, Princess Sophie of the tiny German state of Anhalt-Zerbst.

And when I am duchess, thought Sophie, I shall ride whenever I like.

Had it only been fifty days since Sophie's family had received the longed-for invitation to visit the Russian court? A quick trip to Berlin and the court of King Frederick II of Prussia had them outfitted for the long journey to Russia. Sophie attended a special reception held in her honor. She had never felt so important! Even her mother, Princess Johanna, looked proud.

Afterwards, King Frederick sent Sophie and her mother on their way in a berlin, a covered carriage with a hooded rear seat. Unfortunately, it did not offer much protection from the bitter cold of a Russian winter.

Conditions improved slightly when they entered the Russian city of Riga. They were given a royal sleigh to travel in. It was elegant and much roomier than their berlin had been. The Russian guard wrapped them both in rich sables as they continued on to St. Petersburg, where they received an even grander welcome. Cannons from the nearby Fortress of Peter and Paul fired artillery salvos in honor of their arrival.

Sophie and her mother were treated well in the cosmopolitan city created by Peter the Great. While Sophie's mother enjoyed gossiping with members of the Russian nobility, Sophie toured the city that would someday rival the great European cities of Paris and Berlin. All too soon their wardrobes were replenished and it was time to start for Moscow where Empress Elizabeth and her heir, Grand Duke Peter, awaited them.

"Once again, Sophie was struck by the immensity of the Russian plain. In this country, everything was larger than life: the distances, the cold, the political passions,"[1] writes biographer Henri Troyat.

They traveled day and night because the Empress wanted them present for Peter's birthday. They arrived exhausted on February 9, 1744, the eve of his birthday. Sophie soon forgot her irritation with riding in the sleigh and the accompanying soreness that came from hours and hours of sitting as they traveled through Russia.

Now that she had arrived in the ancient, walled city of Moscow, Sophie found herself a little nervous. She studied the old capital of Russia and marveled at so many grand churches, so unlike her modest Lutheran church at home. The Cathedral Place with its dozens of onion domes glinting in the moonlight made an impressive sight. Sophie had expected a provincial town, but Moscow was anything but.

With her head straight and her eyes focused ahead, Sophie climbed the wooden staircase into the Annenhof Palace at the Kremlin. She nodded and curtsied at the many introductions. She memorized names and filed away information about the dignitaries that she might need later.

"And Sophie, you remember the Grand Duke, Peter of Holstein-Gottorp," her mother announced.

In truth, Sophie barely remembered the slight young man in front of her, although her mother, Princess Johanna, had told her countless times of their meeting at the royal court of the German state of Holstein-Gottorp when she was ten years old. However, Sophie put on her best smile and curtsied.

Peter returned a dignified bow in greeting. "I am glad to see you again, Princess Sophie. How was your journey?"

Sophie wanted to tell him that she was sore from her head to her toes after bouncing around for weeks in the berlin and the sleigh, but a look from her mother said she would be wise not to. "Very well, Your Highness. The Russian countryside is particularly beautiful, as is the capital city," she answered.

"Ah, St. Petersburg. It is my favorite place in all of Russia. My grandfather Peter intended it as a window to the rest of Europe. But surely, the rest of the trip must have been a bore," he smiled.

Sophie was surprised at his candor, although she silently agreed. Maybe being married to this boy wouldn't be so bad after all. Sophie trailed behind her mother and Peter as they entered the state bedchamber. "The little procession traversed a series of rooms filled with dignitaries in brilliant uniform and court ladies whose dresses, as elegant as any at Versailles [the fashionable palace of the French kings just outside of Paris], turned Johanna green with envy,"[2] Troyat comments.

Sophie's first glimpse of Empress Elizabeth impressed her more than all the churches, lands, and gowns she had seen. The majestic woman of thirty-five years was adorned in a silver hoopskirted gown trimmed in gold lace. Sophie could sense the power emanating from this woman who ruled all of Russia.

"The girl had to summon all her presence of mind to keep from fainting before this divinity decked out in all her splendor,"[3] Troyat says. She vowed to learn everything she could from this ruler who had chosen her as consort to her nephew, the grandson of Peter the Great. And like Peter the Great, someday she would be a great ruler.

Sophie would later write in her memoirs, "I believe that in my present course lies the true interest of Russia and that I may hope for great fame for myself in the future."[4]

Her prediction came true. The young German princess would become the first person with no direct ties to Russia to sit on the Russian throne. She would be one of the most powerful rulers Russia ever had, a ruler who made the rest of Europe take notice. As historian Simon Dixon notes, she would become a legend in her own lifetime.

ST. PETERSBURG

Saint Petersburg is one of the world's most beautiful cities. It is designed like a wheel, with its main streets radiating outward from its center and crossing more than 100 islands and 65 rivers and channels. Beautiful palaces and churches adorn this seaport city that has served as Russia's cultural and scientific center since its beginnings.

Located in northwest Russia at the Gulf of Finland, which adjoins the Baltic Sea, the area once belonged to Sweden. It was acquired by Russia during the Great Northern War (1700-1721). Peter the Great, czar of Russia, was happy to have an outlet to the Baltic Sea for travel and trade. He wanted to replace Russia's capital of Moscow with a new capital city in the style of the great cities of Western Europe.

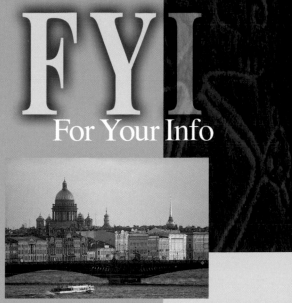

St. Petersburg

With the aid of Dutch and Italian architects, Peter began construction In 1703 on the banks of the Neva River. The first building was the Peter and Paul Fortress that Peter designed himself. He followed with a shipyard and a network of canals and wide streets with plazas. Government buildings and palaces came soon afterward.

St. Petersburg was an aesthetic marvel, but it came at a price. Peasants and convicts were forced to do the work. Millions of tons of soil had to be brought in to bring the site to sea level. Forests were cleared and canals had to be dug. Marshy conditions led to the spread of dysentery and malaria. Thousands of people died from hunger, the cold, and disease.

Russia's new city faced Europe, sending the message that Russia was indeed a world power. Peter the Great named it after his patron saint, St. Peter. In 1712, St. Petersburg was designated the capital of Russia and remained so until 1918. The city would suffer during the Russian Revolution of the early twentieth century and the subsequent communist government of the Soviet Union. It was re-named Petrograd and then Leningrad. Some treasures were lost during this era. The city returned to its original name after the collapse of the Soviet Union in 1990. Today, St. Petersburg is a city rich in Russian culture and history—a window to Europe.

FYI

For Your Info

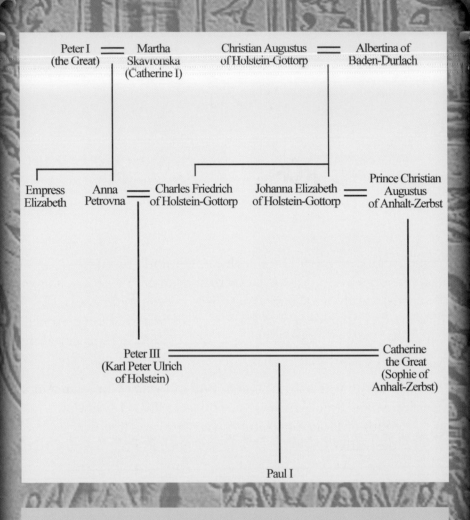

Peter I (the Great) ═══ Martha Skavronska (Catherine I)

Christian Augustus of Holstein-Gottorp ═══ Albertina of Baden-Durlach

Empress Elizabeth

Anna Petrovna ═══ Charles Friedrich of Holstein-Gottorp

Johanna Elizabeth of Holstein-Gottorp ═══ Prince Christian Augustus of Anhalt-Zerbst

Peter III (Karl Peter Ulrich of Holstein) ═══════ Catherine the Great (Sophie of Anhalt-Zerbst)

Paul I

Catherine the Great and her husband, Peter III, were actually cousins. Her mother and his father were siblings.

CHAPTER TWO

THE ROAD TO RUSSIA

Sophie Augusta Fredericka's birth came quietly on April 21, 1729 in the Baltic seaport town of Stettin in German Pomerania. When she was born, Germany was divided into almost 300 independent states, of which Prussia was the most powerful. Some historians believe Stettin may actually have been part of Prussia at this time. This was certainly possible as Sophie's father was an officer in the Prussian military.

Princess Sophie was the first-born child of Prince Christian August of Anhalt-Zerbst and a noblewoman twenty-one years his junior, Johanna Elizabeth of Holstein-Gottorp. Her family called her "Figchen," a derivative of "Sophiechen." At an early age, Sophie felt as if she disappointed everyone by not being a boy. Still, she adored her father, a minor German prince who devoted most of his attention to military service for Prussia. He was a thoughtful man who was content with life in a small province. Sophie thought he was one of the most honorable men she knew.

Only seventeen when her daughter was born, Johanna was used to a more active social life. She had been raised at court by her godmother, dowager Duchess Elisabeth Sophia Maria of Brunswick-Wolfenbüttel. Johanna worried about her plain-looking daughter, who preferred rough physical play and riding horses. No doubt Sophie knew of her mother's disappointment. Johanna would lavish far more attention on the sons who came later, to the virtual exclusion of her daughter.

"I do not know whether I was really ugly as a child, but I remember very well that I was often told I was and for that reason I ought to strive for inward virtues and intelligence,"[1] Catherine would later write in her memoirs.

Neither parent spent much time with Sophie. Instead, a series of women were assigned to watch over the lonely girl. Sophie felt unloved until the day a Frenchwoman named Babet Cardel entered the household. Babet served the family as a nanny and governess for many years and became the person with whom Sophie spent most of her time.

As her first teacher, Babet taught young Sophie to read and to be an independent, intelligent young woman. She also introduced her to the idea of social equality. According to Sophie, Babet was her greatest influence.

"Her enthusiasm for Babet was to remain so lively that even in old age, when writing to Voltaire, she would take pride in calling herself 'the pupil of Mademoiselle Cardel,'"[2] writes Troyat.

Sophie enjoyed learning and read a great deal. She spoke German, and like all nobles of the day, French. Most of her memoirs would be written in French. Even her correspondence was primarily in French. She had no aptitude for music and may have been tone deaf, a fact that she regretted much of her life.

As an intelligent young girl, Sophie was used to expressing her many opinions. She engaged in many disagreements with a Lutheran pastor named Dowe, whom she called "Herr Pastor." He taught religion, history, and geography. No doubt Sophie enjoyed upsetting Herr Pastor with improper questions and disagreeing with him. He often complained of young Sophie's behavior and wanted her punished.

Although she was forced to grow up quickly, it's clear she still enjoyed childish pursuits. "When I was seven years old, all dolls and other playthings were taken from me and I was told that I was a big girl now and they were no longer suitable for me. I have never liked dolls, but nevertheless I liked to play,"[3] she wrote in her memoirs.

The next year, Sophie began accompanying her mother on her regular visits to the court of Brunswick-Wolfenbüttel. Sophie found events of the royal court very interesting and quickly learned how to behave with royalty. In 1739, she met her future husband at court. Peter had been born Karl Peter Ulrich of Holstein-Gottorp to one of Peter the Great's daughters and a brother of Johanna's. That made him a cousin.

There are differing accounts on what Sophie thought of their first meeting. Some reports are that she found Peter a handsome and well-mannered 11-year-old. Others said Sophie viewed him as a sickly, boring boy. Peter's father had recently died, and it's not clear if this incident may have affected Peter's behavior or appearance at this first meeting.

No doubt Sophie's curiosity was piqued at meeting the grandson of Peter the Great, a boy destined for an important royal position. The meeting, however, probably meant more to concerned adults intent on matchmaking.

As Sophie grew older, her mother recognized her daughter's sharp mind and began working to make a match for her brilliant daughter. Peter was her first choice. King Frederick II of Prussia considered this match to be advantageous to him and encouraged Johanna's efforts.

In the 1740s, Empress Elizabeth had begun searching for a wife for Peter, her nephew and successor. Although she was rumored to be married to a commoner, Elizabeth had no children of her own. As the youngest daughter of Peter the Great, she had staged a successful coup in 1741 to take the throne from a distant relative, Anna Leopoldovna, who was acting as regent for her infant son Ivan VI.

The German princess, Sophie, was a sentimental favorite. Elizabeth had been engaged to another of Johanna's brothers, Karl

Augustus of Holstein-Gottorp, before he died unexpectedly of smallpox in 1727.

Empress Elizabeth summoned Sophie and her mother to Russia in late 1743. A banquet honoring the now important young princess was held in Berlin before they left. King Frederick advised her mother about the alliance. He saw it as a way to further Prussia's cause with the Russian court. Sophie had already said good-bye to her father, not realizing that she would never see him again. He died in 1747.

Soon after arriving in Russia, Sophie took ill with a high fever. The Empress wanted the physicians to "bleed" her through a common practice of applying leeches to the skin. Sophie's mother refused. It was one of many disagreements between the two women. Luckily, Sophie had recovered by her fifteenth birthday.

Peter was an unhappy young man. His aunt had taken him from his home and changed his name to Peter Fedorovich. He made no secret of the fact that he hated everything Russian. Sophie wasn't certain of Peter's feelings for her. "He seemed to like me; but I can neither say that I liked him nor that I disliked him. I only know how to obey, and my mother had to marry me; I believe in truth however that the Russian crown meant more to me than he,"[4] she said in her memoirs.

Elizabeth gave her approval of a union between Sophie and Peter. Sophie took to her adopted homeland quickly.

"In Petersburg I led a very retired life. I used the six weeks during which I was alone with my mother for the study of Russian, which I had already begun to understand and to speak. I wrote the Empress several times in this language which gave her great joy,"[5] she wrote of this period.

Catherine also studied the Orthodox Church. She converted from Lutheranism to the Russian Orthodox Church on June 28, 1744. She was christened Ekaterina (Catherine) Alekseevna. Her christening was followed by a betrothal ceremony. Grand Duchess Catherine and Grand Duke Peter were now officially engaged.

PETER THE GREAT

Peter I, more commonly known as Peter the Great, was one of Russia's most famous rulers. He was the czar and later, the first emperor of Russia. He is generally credited with initiating the change of Russia into one of the great European powers.

*Peter I
(Peter the Great)*

Born in Moscow in 1672, Peter became czar at the age of 10. Czar (sometimes spelled as tsar) was a Byzantine term first used by Ivan III during the 1300s to show supreme rule. It was derived from the Roman word Caesar. Although he ruled with his half-siblings for a time, Peter became Russia's sole ruler in 1696.

Peter had always been interested in military affairs and in the West. At a young age, he made contact with Europeans living in Moscow and learned about commerce and government. In the late 1600s, he traveled through Europe disguised as a sailor. He brought back many ideas and experts to modernize the military and reorganize the government. Under Peter's leadership, Russia gained territory on the Baltic Sea. This opened up trade opportunities. He introduced European clothing and customs, factories, and architecture to Russia.

Peter imposed high taxes on Russia to finance his military campaigns and reforms. He forced people to work against their will in his mines, factories, and building projects. The number of serfs, a type of slave, grew under Peter's rule.

Almost seven feet tall, Peter was very strong and dealt harshly with those who opposed him. He was said to be more comfortable talking over a beer with foreign sailors than dressing up and conducting matters at court. Upon victory in the Great Northern War, which began in 1700 and ended in 1721, the Russian Empire was formed. Czar Peter declared himself Peter the Great, Emperor of all Russia.

Catherine never lost an opportunity during her reign to speak admirably of Peter the Great. Her ties to the Russian throne were not very strong. Being compared to Peter the Great wouldn't hurt.

Peter III was the grandson of Peter the Great. Empress Elizabeth picked her nephew to succeed her as ruler when she died. He was not a popular ruler during his short rule.

BIOGRAPHY FROM ANCIENT CIVILIZATIONS
LEGENDS, FOLKLORE, AND STORIES OF ANCIENT WORLDS

CHAPTER
THREE

THE NEW EMPRESS

The wedding between Catherine and Peter was to take place August 21, 1745 at the Kazan Cathedral in St. Petersburg. In her memoirs, Catherine describes rising at six that morning in order to prepare in the Empress's apartments. Once Catherine was wearing her exquisite wedding dress of silver glacé with silver embroidery, Empress Elizabeth laid a grand ducal crown on Catherine's head.

The wedding was a lavish affair with no expense spared. The English ambassador described the ten days of festivities as the grandest thing he had ever seen. Soon afterwards, Johanna was told she could return home.

Grand Duchess Catherine was soon well-liked at court. She was intelligent and charming. Studying the imperial court, she took note of the most influential people. But life at court soon changed for Catherine. She hadn't counted on being watched by Elizabeth's secret police. The Empress, who knew only too well about overthrowing those in power, had everyone watched. Peter didn't seem to mind much. But Catherine became more isolated. Even her mail was opened.

Worried that people were spreading lies about her to Empress Elizabeth, Catherine asked to speak to the Empress alone, but was refused. "Her dislike of me increased from year to year, although my aim has always been to do her pleasure in everything,"[1] Catherine wrote.

Catherine spent much of her time riding and hunting. She also continued to read. She learned about the rulers of ancient Rome and studied Machiavelli's account of power struggles among Italian princes of the Renaissance. She became familiar with the politics of the court and the rest of Russia. Empress Elizabeth may have been the ruler, but women were generally treated as the property of their fathers or husbands in Russia. Men were allowed to beat and even kill women for misbehaving. If a woman fought back, she was punished. The punishment might consist of being sent to a convent. But it wasn't unheard of for women to have their noses cut off or be buried up to their neck in a pit until they died from thirst.

Unfortunately, the match between Catherine and her husband was far from ideal. Peter had a reputation for being difficult. He cared little for politics or learning. Catherine thought that Peter was rather childlike with his talk about his playthings and his toy soldiers. It was rumored that Peter was unable or unwilling to consummate the marriage and reportedly humiliated her in front of others. Still, Empress Elizabeth encouraged the two to have a baby in order to carry on the royal lineage.

After nine years of marriage and two miscarriages, Catherine gave birth to a son, Paul Petrovich Romanov, on September 20, 1754. His real father may have been a Russian officer, Sergei Saltykov. It was one of many love affairs that Catherine had during her lifetime. In later years, she reportedly had a daughter and another son, but neither apparently lived very long.

Catherine gave birth to Paul next to the Empress's rooms. As soon as he was born, he was taken to Elizabeth. "The birth of the royal heir was, of course, a patriotic and religious event of greatest magnitude. Cannons boomed salutes from every fortress and warship, the palaces were draped with flags, bells rang praises from the gold and multicolored

Empress Elizabeth (shown here) was a ruthless leader and the youngest daughter of Peter the Great. Elizabeth overthrew a sister and nephew in 1741 to take control of Russia. She trusted few people and was said to have spies and secret police watching everyone at court. Childless, she arranged for another nephew, Peter, to succeed her.

domed belfries, and in the churches the Russian people gathered for prayer and thanksgiving,"[2] writes historian Robert Coughlan.

None of this attention was focused on Catherine. Not only was she ignored after a difficult birth, but she was also not given any time to bond with her son. This may have contributed to the poor relationship the two had for the remainder of Catherine's life. Elizabeth apparently no longer had any use for Catherine. The Empress kept Paul, now second in line for the throne, with her until her death.

Late in 1761, Elizabeth took ill. She died on Christmas Day. "The death of the Empress Elizabeth plunged all Russians into deep mourning, especially all good patriots, because they saw in her successor a ruler of violent character and narrow intellect, who hated and despised the Russians, did not know his country, was incompetent to do hard work, avaricious and wasteful, and gave himself up wholly to his desires and to those who slavishly flattered him,"[3] Catherine commented.

Peter ascended to the throne and became Peter III of Russia, and was an unpopular ruler. His ascension took place during the Seven Years' War. Russia, along with Austria and France, had been fighting against Prussia. Peter made no secret of the fact that he preferred Prussian ways and greatly admired their ruler, Frederick II. Peter aligned himself with Prussia and signed a peace agreement. He also engineered a peace between Prussia and Sweden.

Peter delighted in taking land away from the Russian Orthodox Church. Rumors began circulating that Peter wanted to divorce Catherine or imprison her. He may even have considered having her murdered. However, he knew that public support for his wife was high.

The Russian military viewed Peter as foolish. In addition to pulling the military from their successful attacks against Prussia, he reorganized the Russian army in the Prussian style, complete with similar uniforms.

Since the time of Peter the Great, the Russian czars, emperors and empresses had absolute power. Only something drastic could stop them.

The army arrested Peter on June 28, 1762. On the same day, Catherine arrived in St. Petersburg amid cheers from the public. The Imperial Guard and other troops proclaimed her the ruler. Peter was forced to resign after only six months as czar. A little over a week later on July 6, Peter was found dead. The official cause of death was listed as a hemorrhoid attack with violent colic. However, it was strongly suspected that he was murdered by one of Catherine's supporters. Catherine's current lover was a member of the Imperial Guard, Grigory Orlov. His brother, Aleksei, was also in the Imperial Guard and had been assigned to watch Peter. It's possible that Aleksei strangled Peter or poisoned him.

Catherine denied any part in her husband's death. While it's certain that Catherine had a hand in the plot to overthrow her husband and take over as ruler of Russia, there is no proof that she ordered his death. But had Peter lived, he could have eventually challenged her right to rule Russia. The circumstances of Peter's death caused even more dissension between Catherine and her son, Paul.

Peter was quickly forgotten as Catherine took the throne. Her coronation on September 22, 1762 was held in the same location as other czars and empresses: the magnificent onion-domed Cathedral of the Assumption in Moscow's Kremlin. No expense was spared to make this a coronation people would remember. She commissioned a jeweler to redesign the imperial crown. Three thousand workers erected impressive gates in Moscow for the event. At the age of 33 years and having lived more than half her life—eighteen years—in her adopted homeland, she was crowned Catherine II, Empress of Russia. It was the realization of a long-held ambition.

"Only months after her coronation, she boasted to the French ambassador that her sights had been set on sole rulership from the moment she set foot in Russia in 1744. In memoirs begun in 1771, she claimed that it was the prospect of an earthly crown, first dreamt of in childhood that had sustained her through the oppressive isolation she endured at Elizabeth's court in the 1740s and 1750s,"[1] writes historian Simon Dixon.

Catherine seemed born to take the Russian crown. Unlike other monarchs of the day, Catherine went out among the people instead of hiding behind palace walls. The early days of her rule found her traveling in an open sleigh with a minimum of attendants, which impressed foreign dignitaries. When she walked to church, people from the street wanted to walk with her. According to biographer Henri Troyat, the public referred to her as the "Little Mother."

Her inspiration wasn't Elizabeth as much as it was Peter the Great. Like him, she wanted to introduce great changes, but she believed persuasion was a better tool than the force he had used. She used her considerable charm on her critics, whether they were a Russian commoner, a philosopher of the Enlightenment, or a Western official.

SEVEN YEARS' WAR

FYI
For Your Info

Madame de Pompadour

Many of the wars in eighteenth century Europe were fought over land and the Seven Years' War was no exception. Both Prussia and Austria were interested in a small piece of land—the province of Silesia. Frederick II, King of Prussia, had seized the province in 1740 from Austria. Maria Theresa, Austria's ruler, was determined to regain Silesia. She tried unsuccessfully twice to regain Silesia during the War of the Austrian Succession (1740–48).

Located in north-central Europe, Prussia was the most powerful of the German states during the eighteenth and nineteenth centuries. With the backing of his strong military forces, Frederick had the goal of expanding Prussian territory. As Austria planned its third attempt to regain Silesia, Frederick found out and invaded nearby Saxony. And the Seven Years' War began.

Prussia was aided solely by Britain. Austria had the support of most of the rest of Europe. Its two most important allies were France—which came about through Louis XV's powerful and influential mistress, Madame de Pompadour—and Empress Elizabeth of Russia. Together, these three women—Maria Theresa, Madame de Pompadour and Elizabeth—became known as the League of the Three Petticoats. Eventually, most of Europe became involved in the conflict.

By 1762, Prussia's resources were exhausted. It looked like they might lose the war. However, when Peter III ascended to the Russian throne, he made peace with Prussia, a country he had long admired. He also mediated a peace between Prussia and Sweden. The Seven Years' war ended with Prussia keeping control of Silesia.

But the desire for more territory led Britain and France to take the struggle to three other continents as they fought over the American colonies, West Indies, India, and Africa. The British won most of the battles and became the world leader in acquiring overseas colonies.

Catherine the Great (shown here) introduced many reforms to Russian government. She was able to reduce Russia's debt. She also opened schools and encouraged education.

CHAPTER
FOUR

RUSSIAN REFORMS

Catherine ascended to the throne during a very difficult period. Russia faced huge debts. It was a large country that had been managed poorly. Ineffective administrators and corruption were the norms. No one in her Senate could even tell her how many towns Russia had. One of her first duties was to appoint a new cabinet and ministers. She chose people she could trust, and she rewarded them for their loyalty.

Four secretaries were kept busy all day, but no one worked harder than the new Empress. She rose before 6:00 a.m. most mornings. Fifteen-hour workdays were common for her. She channeled her enormous amount of energy into reading reports, issuing edicts, and familiarizing herself with everything having to do with Russia.

Catherine reversed the unpopular decisions that Peter had instituted in his brief rule, except in regard to Prussia. She didn't resume the war. It's likely that she looked favorably on Prussia. Her father had served in the Prussian army and its ruler, Frederick II, had been instrumental in arranging her marriage to Peter.

She did focus on increasing Russia's wealth, starting with agriculture. Experts studied soil conditions and incorporated modern farming methods. She began mining operations and trained miners in silver mining. The Free Economic Society for the Encouragement of Agriculture and Husbandry, established in 1765, was formed to improve agriculture and industry through modernization.

Catherine encouraged the continued fur trade in Siberia, an area she realized held great natural wealth. It was dotted with copper, gold, iron and silver mines and other valuable resources.

Whenever possible, she turned to experts from the West. She called on Sir Charles Knowles, an English admiral, to build her shipyards and ports. When experts couldn't come to Russia, she sent Russians elsewhere to study. Unlike Peter the Great's pilgrimage to the West, Catherine never left Russia. However, she did travel throughout Russia for many months to survey her empire's vast lands. She then instructed administrators to develop accurate maps and census reports.

The number of factories manufacturing and producing goods more than tripled during Catherine's reign. Soon, Russia was exporting timber, hemp, leather, furs, linens, and iron. She abolished export duties and introduced paper money. By 1765, Russia's budget deficit had been turned into a surplus.

Catherine further won the hearts of the nobility by first reducing, and then abolishing, the service obligation for the nobility that Peter the Great had begun. The Russian nobility was free to adopt the ways of the French-speaking leisure class of the European courts.

The Empress believed Peter the Great had been correct in trying to westernize Russia, and she continued those efforts. She, herself, was influenced heavily by writers of the Enlightenment, in particular Voltaire and Denis Diderot. These modern writers proposed radical ideas for the time, such as basic rights for all people.

One of the rights that Catherine supported was education. Outside of church officials and a few nobles, most Russians were illiterate. In 1782, she created the Commission on National Education to establish more schools, train teachers, and provide textbooks. She mandated that schools be set up in all provinces and district towns. Although serfs were expected to work the land, she encouraged other children to attend school. The Smolny Institute for Girls became the first girls' school. In 1783, a teachers' college, the Russian Academy of Letters, opened its doors. Catherine further contributed to the education effort by writing a text, *Russian Primer for the Instruction of Youth.*

She was delighted when Voltaire commended her. "One must certainly pay tribute to your Imperial Majesty for your excellent schools for boys and girls,"[1] he wrote.

Another concern was health care. She established a medical school in 1763, believing that Russia should be able to produce its own physicians and medicines. Infectious diseases were a particular concern, even more so when a plague in 1771 killed approximately 125,000 in the central provinces; about 55,000 died in Moscow. Smallpox vaccination was introduced. When Catherine received her vaccination in 1768, the occasion was designated a national feast day.

Russia needed the most work done in its government and policies, which Catherine considered quite backward. She formed a legislative assembly to discuss Russia's new government. Six hundred people from throughout Russia were summoned to Moscow in 1767 to discuss the new Russian government.

But first, Catherine laid out an outline of her ideal government in her memoirs. "I read and wrote two years and said not a word for a year and a half, but followed my own judgment and feelings, with a sincere striving for the service, the honor, and the happiness of the empire, and with the desire to bring about in all respects the highest welfare of people and of things, of all in general and each individual in particular,"[2] she wrote.

In practice, she presented her thoughts to this assembly in a volume that contained hundreds of "instructions." She gave the book the name of *Bolshoi Nakaz*, or *The INSTRUCTIONS to the Commissioners for Composing a New Code of Laws.* When it was published throughout Europe, it was simply called *The Great Instruction.* The philosopher Voltaire gave it high praise and she became known as the "philosophic sovereign." The first chapter defined Russia as a European state due to the introduction and adoption of European ways during the reign of Peter the Great.

Catherine called for freedoms the Russian people were unfamiliar with, such as freedom of religion and freedom of expression. She proposed that government should not be about denying personal liberty, but promoting the greatest good. This was evident in her first instruction, in which she wrote "The Christian Law teaches us to do mutual good to one another, as much as we possibly can."[3]

She even wrote about serfs, whom she wanted freed. She later had to back away from this issue. She felt the results of ending serfdom would result in chaos and the loss of support from Russia's nobility.

The assembly met for almost 17 months until the Ottoman Empire declared war on Russia in 1768. A great deal of information was exchanged and debated. For the first time in Russia, the common man was allowed to take part in a discussion of ideas of how the government should operate.

Russia was often at war with neighboring countries, including Prussia, Turkey, Poland, and Sweden. Like Peter the Great, Catherine wanted Russia to grow. Russia gained about 200,000 square miles of land during Catherine's reign, mainly to the west and the south. Russia defeated the Ottoman Empire (Turkey) in two wars (1768-1774 and 1787-1792), which added to its holdings. After only nine years of independence from the Ottoman Empire, Russia annexed the Crimea in 1783.

Russia also gained nearly all of modern-day Belarus, Lithuania, and Ukraine from Poland. In 1772, Poland was split among Russia, Prussia, and Austria. Later partitions of Poland occurred in 1793 and 1795. The

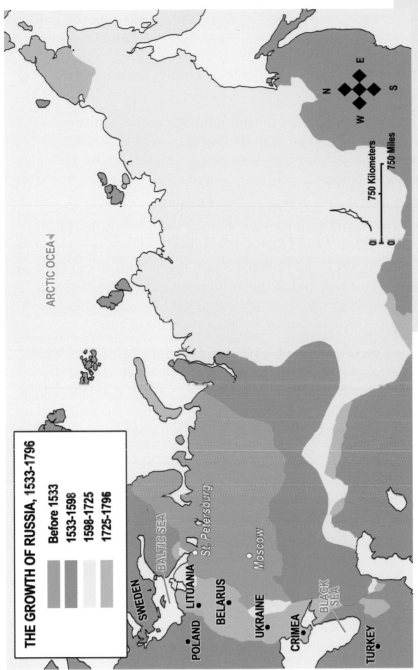

THE GROWTH OF RUSSIA, 1533-1796

- Before 1533
- 1533-1598
- 1598-1725
- 1725-1796

ARCTIC OCEAN

SWEDEN

BALTIC SEA

St. Petersburg

LITHUANIA

POLAND

BELARUS

Moscow

UKRAINE

CRIMEA

BLACK SEA

TURKEY

N
W   E
S

750 Kilometers
0

750 Miles
0

During Catherine the Great's reign, Russia gained about 200,000 miles (518,000 km). Through many battles, Russia gained parts of the Ottoman Empire (Turkey), Crimea, Poland, and Sweden. These gains led to a larger population of people and access to better sea routes for trade.

third partition erased Poland from the map. More land along the Baltic Sea was acquired from Sweden in 1787 and 1788. Catherine established control of the northern coast of the Black Sea, something Peter the Great had been unable to do. This opened a better trade route for Russia

These significant increases in land holdings resulted in seven million more people being added to the population of Russia. Catherine also encouraged European migration to Russia. Almost 40,000 Germans settled in southern Russia.

Wars are never easy, and Catherine recognized that truth. She believed that a swift and strong attack yielded the best results. One of her most trusted advisors was Grigory Potemkin, to whom she wrote: "If you want to remove the stone from my heart, if you want to calm my spasms, quickly send a courier to the armies and permit the land and naval forces to begin operations as soon as possible or you'll drag out the war much longer, which, of course, neither you nor I desire."[4]

She made Potemkin the governor-general of the Ukraine. Under his leadership, army reforms contributed to Russia's conquest of the Crimea. He also oversaw development of Russian ports and ships along the Black Sea. For his efforts, Catherine made him first a count, and later, a prince.

SERFDOM

Alexander II

FYI
For Your Info

A serf was a type of peasant in Europe and parts of Asia. He was similar to a tenant farmer in that he lived in his own house on a large estate. But the serf had to pay the landlord or owner of the land a heavy rent of money, farm products, or labor. Unlike slaves, who were owned by people, serfs were essentially "owned" by the land. If a piece of land was sold, the serfs stayed with the land.

Serfs were given inferior status in society and had few legal rights. They could not give testimony in court, dispose of personal property, or get married without special permission. Perhaps the main mark of a serf was his restricted movement. He could not leave his landlord's property or his village without permission.

The concept of serfdom developed after the collapse of the Roman Empire. Peasants who served a landowner were called *servi*, which gradually evolved into *serfs*. As economic conditions improved in the 1100's and 1200's, many serfs in Western Europe bought their freedom or ran away to cities. Serf revolts occurred in many places. Essentially, serfdom ended in Western Europe by the 1500s.

Serfdom spread to Eastern Europe around the 1300s and became official in Russia during the reign of Czar Ivan IV in the middle of the seventeenth century. During the following century, their freedom of movement was reduced but they still had some rights. The status of serfs worsened under the rule of Peter the Great, as most of their rights were stripped away. While serfdom was fading elsewhere, it actually increased in Russia during the eighteenth century. This development coincided with an increased demand for grain from Western Europe. Nobles and other landlords made heavy demands for peasant labor. The living conditions for serfs improved during the reigns of Alexander I and Nicholas I. They were freed by Alexander II in 1861.

Francois Marie Arouet (shown here) was
better known by the pen name of Voltaire.
He was one of the chief voices in the
Enlightenment Movement. Catherine and
Voltaire corresponded often.

CHAPTER
FIVE

PATRON OF THE ARTS

Catherine loved things of beauty. She is credited with bringing this beauty to Russia through her interest in arts and culture. As in other areas, she believed that Western Europe had the most to offer.

Due to her interest in the Enlightenment movement, Catherine became friendly with many European writers and even financed translations of their works so that these works would be available to more Russians. One of the writers Catherine admired was Voltaire, with whom she corresponded until his death. He was full of praise for Catherine too and referred to her as the "Northern Star."

"Your Imperial Majesty has found a path of glory hitherto unknown to all other monarchs," he wrote. "None had ever resolved to bestow bounties seven or eight hundred leagues from his realm. You have truly become the benefactress of Europe; and you have won more subjects by your magnanimity than others can by force of arms."[1]

Catherine boasted that she owned 38,000 books. These included the libraries of Diderot and Voltaire, which she obtained after their deaths. She started the St. Petersburg Public Library. Russia's first private printing presses were established, giving rise to the publication of literary journals. Catherine even contributed to these journals in addition to writing plays, adapting Shakespeare to Russian, and composing operas. She wrote in both Russian and French. She built the Hermitage Theatre so that her plays and operas could be performed. Today, it is the scene of performances from the world's foremost opera and dance companies.

Catherine brought foreign artists to Russia. In addition to influencing local artists, she commissioned projects from these famed artists. Perhaps the most well-known is the Bronze Horseman statue in St. Petersburg by French sculptor Etienne-Maurice Falconet. It is a statue of Peter the Great that shows him as a Roman hero atop a horse. The horse is stepping on a snake, which represents enemies of Russia. The statue stands on a cliff-shaped piece of red granite and faces the Neva River. Its inscription reads "To Peter the First from Catherine the Second."

Russian artists were sent to Paris, Amsterdam, and Florence to further their education. Artists Vladimir Borovikovsky and Ivan Argunov became known for their portraits, leading to a boom in miniature portraits in Russia. The Imperial Academy of the Arts even added a class on miniature painting. As much as she liked art, Catherine did not like to sit for her portrait. Portraits rarely captured the true Catherine. She was a striking woman, although she gained a great deal of weight in her later years.

The Imperial Porcelain Factory in St. Petersburg boomed under Catherine's direction. For her coronation ceremonies, she issued a directive to the factory, ordering them to send their best porcelain to Moscow. She believed the factory could make a profit at producing artistic decorative porcelain. At the time of Catherine's death, it was producing nearly 40,000 high-quality pieces of art every year.

Catherine also collected art. It was not single pieces of art that appealed to her as much as entire collections. She startled leaders all over Europe in 1764 with her first major acquisition. She purchased 225 paintings, mostly by Italian and Flemish old masters, from a Berlin merchant named Johann Ernst Gotzowsky. Gotzowsky had originally planned on selling them to the Prussian king Frederick II. But the

Prussian treasury had been exhausted by the Seven Years' War and Catherine took advantage of the opportunity. In the years to come, she continued her purchases, acquiring major collections from men such as Baron Pierre Crozat and Lord Robert Walpole.

Her growing collection needed a home. Construction had begun on the Hermitage, a wing of the Winter Palace, in 1754 in St. Petersburg. With a thousand rooms, the palace was an impressive structure built of jasper, malachite, marble, and gold. Four of the rooms were filled with collections of books and prints plus two rooms of natural history. Now a museum open to the public, the State Hermitage contains one of the world's greatest art collections.

Catherine was often criticized for the amount of money she spent. Did she hope that exposure to the arts along with reforms would better the lives of Russians? Many Russians, particularly serfs and peasants, were worse off during Catherine's reign. To finance her purchases, she had to raise taxes. The additional burden also raised discontent.

Instead of helping, her reforms often widened the gulf between the nobles and peasants. While their empress was building beautiful palaces, the peasants saw that they were poorer than ever. Serfs had more work than ever. When Catherine raised the taxes of the nobles, the nobles turned around and required more taxes from their serfs.

In 1773, a Cossack (a member of a Slavic people living in southern Russia) named Yemelyan Pugachev started a revolt of angry peasants intent on overthrowing Catherine. He claimed that he was Peter III and said that he would become the ruler who would end serfdom. The peasant revolt grew to include 30,000 armed men and spread throughout the Volga region, attacking landlords. It almost reached Moscow before being crushed by the military. By early 1775, Pugachev had been captured and publicly executed.

When Voltaire asked about Pugachev, Catherine replied: "Marquis Pugachev, whom you mention again in your letter of December 16th, lived a villain and will die a coward."[2]

Catherine introduced a new system of local self-government to help prevent future rebellions like the one initiated by Pugachev. She emphasized decentralization to give local governments more control. Catherine then tightened the landowners' control over the serfs.

In 1789, Catherine heard news of the French Revolution. Like other nobles throughout Europe, she was horrified and frightened. She became even more alarmed when she learned of the beheading of the French King Louis the XVI and his wife Marie Antoinette several years later. Interestingly, it was ideas proposed by the Enlightenment movement that she had long supported that fueled the Revolution and led to the end of the monarchy in France. Catherine broke off all ties with France and had the Russian police monitor all French-speaking foreigners.

She became more conservative in her rule in later years, even reversing some of her earlier policies. Although she had long promoted freedom of expression, she changed after the peasant revolts and the French Revolution. She censored any literature that criticized her or her rule. In 1790, author Alexander Radishchev published a book called *A Journey from St. Petersburg to Moscow* in which he criticized autocratic rule and the concept of serfdom. He was condemned to death in 1790, only to have his sentence commuted to ten years' exile in Siberia. Siberia in the far north had been used since the 1600s as a place to punish people due to its extreme cold and barrenness. In 1792, Catherine sentenced publisher Nikolai Novikov without a trial to 15 years in prison for publishing unauthorized books.

The Empress continued to have disagreements with her son, Paul. Russian monarchs were allowed to choose their successor. Because she had a hard time with Paul, Catherine had planned for her grandson, Alexander, to succeed her. But before she could put these changes in writing, she died on November 6, 1796, probably of a stroke. Her body was embalmed and lay in state for three weeks. Thousands of mourners slowly passed by to honor her.

She was succeeded by her son, Paul. At his orders, the body of his father, Peter III, was taken out of the tomb where it had lain for more than 30 years. Peter was reburied next to Catherine. Those two people, who disliked each other so much in life, were reunited in death.

She was buried in the Cathedral of St. Peter and St. Paul in St. Petersburg under an epitaph she had written that summarized her life:

> *In the year 1744 she went to Russia to marry Peter III.*
> *At the age of fourteen she made the threefold resolution, to please her Consort, Elizabeth, and the Nation.*
> *She neglected nothing in order to succeed in this.*
> *Eighteen years of tediousness and solitude caused her to read many books.*
> *When she had ascended the throne of Russia, she wished to do good and tried to bring happiness, freedom, and prosperity to her subjects.*
> *She forgave easily and hated no one.*
> *She was good-natured and easy-going; she had a cheerful temperament, republican sentiments, and a kind heart.*
> *She had friends.*
> *Work was easy for her; she loved sociability and the arts.[1]*

After Peter the Great died, Russia had a succession of czars and empresses that led to little progress. When Catherine the Great ascended the Russian throne, Russia once again had a strong ruler for thirty-four years, longer than nearly everyone who had preceded her. Catherine the Great had high ideals for Russia. She believed that the answers lay in the governments, philosophies, and culture of Western Europe. During her reign, Russia truly became a European country. This once-plain, minor German princess worked tirelessly to institute reforms and modernize Russia. Catherine the Great began a process of education, arts, and government that made Russia a world power that continued to grow even stronger in the nineteenth century.

FYI
For Your Info

THE ENLIGHTENMENT

The Enlightenment was a movement in Europe that began at the end of the seventeenth century. It suggested that everything in the universe could be explained by reason. This period was also known as The Age of Reason. Its roots came from the study of the ancient Greek philosophers, the Renaissance, and a scientific revolution.

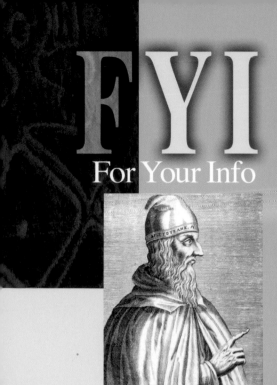

Aristotle

Ancient philosophers like Aristotle were the first to talk about the regular way in which the natural world and natural law operated. The Renaissance focused on classical learning and a de-emphasis on the church. Soon afterwards, a scientific revolution developed in which amazing discoveries were made by men like Francis Bacon, Nicolaus Copernicus, and Galileo.

The Enlightenment drew strongly from these scientific and mathematical discoveries. Perhaps the most significant influence came from Isaac Newton. His theories explained the universe, which was the goal of the Enlightenment philosophers.

According to the Enlightenment, reason led to truth. By using observation and experimentation, new truths about human nature could be learned. Leaders of the movement included philosophers Denis Diderot, Jean-Jacques Rousseau, and John Locke. They believed that humans had advantages over all other creatures because they can reason. Additionally, each person had a rational will that made it possible to make and carry out plans. People who acted impulsively were said to do so because of inadequate education. Education, along with free speech, were important concepts of the Enlightenment.

The ideals of the Enlightenment spread to religion, psychology, ethics, and literature. They had a profound effect on law and politics. The emphasis on social justice and natural rights sowed the seeds for the Revolutionary War in America and the French Revolution. Enlightenment writers shared their knowledge in *Encyclopedie*, a famous magazine that was published for many years.

The Enlightenment attempted to replace a religious world view with one of human reason. It failed because there is so much in human behavior and emotions that cannot be explained. Yet the Age of Enlightenment offered the world lasting ideals and knowledge. Advances were made in anatomy, astronomy, chemistry, mathematics, and physics.

Chronology

Pope Gregory XIII introduced the Gregorian calendar in 1582. For most of Europe, this replaced the Julian calendar which was 10 days earlier. Russia kept the Julian calendar until 1918; therefore all dates are based on the Julian calendar.

1729 Born in Stettin, Pomerania on April 21

1739 Meets Grand Duke Peter

1744 Arrives in Moscow at the request of Empress Elizabeth to become betrothed to Grand Duke Peter; studies the Orthodox religion and becomes Catherine Alekseevna

1745 Marries Grand Duke Peter, the heir to the Russian throne

1747 Father, Christian Augustus of Anhalt-Zerbst, dies

1754 Gives birth to Paul, the future Emperor of Russia

1760 Death of Johanna, her mother

1761 Empress Elizabeth dies on December 25; Peter III is crowned czar

1762 Supported by the Imperial Guard, overthrows Peter and becomes Catherine II; Peter III dies while being imprisoned

1763 Begins to collect art from all over Europe and exhibits it at the newly built Hermitage

1764 Adopts principles of free schools for boys and girls, which begins a period of European-style education

1765 Establishes Free Economic Society for the Encouragement of Agriculture and Husbandry

1767 Influenced by the French Enlightenment, forms a commission for legal reform and publishes the Instructions

1768 Receives smallpox vaccination

1775 Reforms the provincial and urban administrations

1783 Annexes the Crimea

1789 Begins to undo many of her liberal reforms because of the French Revolution

1796 Dies in St. Petersburg on November 6; her son Paul becomes emperor

Timeline
in History

1672	Peter the Great is born.
1687	Sir Isaac Newton publishes his theories on gravity.
1688	France begins colonizing Louisiana.
1694	Francois Marie Arouet, who later takes the pen name of Voltaire, is born.
1700	The Great Northern War begins; the conflict lasts until 1721 and results in Russia gaining territory.
1703	Peter the Great founds the city of St. Petersburg.
1725	Peter the Great dies; he is succeeded by his wife, Catherine I.
1726	Voltaire is exiled from France for three years due to his writing.
1727	Peter II, grandson of Peter the Great, assumes the throne.
1730	Empress Anna takes the throne after the death of Peter II.
1741	Elizabeth I stages a coup and becomes Empress of Russia.
1756	The Seven Years' War begins.
1761	Empress Elizabeth dies on December 25 and Catherine's husband ascends to the Russian throne as Peter III.
1762	Peter III signs a treaty with Frederick II of Prussia.
1768	The Ottoman Empire declares war on Russia.
1772	Russia meets with Prussia and Austria with the objective of partitioning Poland.

Timeline
in History

1773	Cossack Yemelyan Pugachev leads a peasant revolt in the Volga River Basin.
1775	Pugachev is captured, put on trial and executed.
1776	The American Revolution begins with the signing of the Declaration of Independence.
1777	The future Czar Alexander I is born.
1778	Voltaire dies.
1789	The French Revolution begins with the storming of the Bastille prison.
1795	Poland is partitioned for the third and final time; it disappears from the map of Europe until 1918.
1796	Catherine's son Paul becomes czar.
1799	Napoleon comes to power in France.
1801	Czar Paul is assassinated; he is succeeded by Alexander I.
1812	Emperor Napoleon invades Russia; his army captures Moscow but is soon driven out with heavy losses.
1825	Alexander I dies; he is succeeded by Nicholas I.
1837	The first railroad in Russia opens.
1852	Louis Napoleon becomes French emperor.
1853	The Crimean War, in which Great Britain and France fight Russia, begins; it ends three years later.

Chapter Notes

CHAPTER ONE   THE ARRIVAL

1. Henri Troyat, *Catherine the Great,* translated by Joan Pinkham (New York: E. P. Dutton, 1977), p. 18.

2. Ibid., p. 19.

3. Ibid., p. 20.

4. Catherine II, *Memoirs of Catherine the Great*, translated by Katharine Anthony (New York: Tudor Publishing Company, 1935), p. 251.

CHAPTER TWO   THE ROAD TO RUSSIA

1. Catherine II, *Memoirs of Catherine the Great*, translated by Katharine Anthony (New York: Tudor Publishing Company, 1935), p. 13.

2. Henri Troyat, *Catherine the Great,* translated by Joan Pinkham (New York: E. P. Dutton, 1977), p. 4.

3. Catherine II, *Memoirs*, p. 7.

4. Ibid., p. 44

5. Ibid., p. 236.

CHAPTER THREE   THE NEW EMPRESS

1. Catherine II, *Memoirs of Catherine the Great*, translated by Katharine Anthony (New York: Tudor Publishing Company, 1935), p. 251.

2. Robert Coughlan, *Elizabeth and Catherine: Empresses of the Russias* (New York: G. P. Putnam, 1974), p. 113.

3. Catherine II, *Memoirs of Catherine the Great*, translated by Katharine Anthony (New York: Tudor Publishing Company, 1935), p. 263.

Chapter Notes

4. Simon Dixon, *Catherine the Great* (London: Pearson Education Limited, 2001) p. 23.

CHAPTER FOUR   RUSSIAN REFORMS

1. Voltaire and Catherine the Great, *Voltaire and Catherine the Great: Selected Correspondence*, translated by Anthony Lentin (Cambridge, England: Oriental Research Partners, 1974), p. 146.

2. Catherine II, *Memoirs of Catherine the Great*, translated by Katharine Anthony (New York: Tudor Publishing Company, 1935), p. 306.

3. W. F. Reddaway, editor, *Documents of Catherine the Great* (*Correspondence with Voltaire and Instructions of 1767*) (Cambridge, England: Cambridge University Press, 1931), p. 215.

4. Douglas Smith, editor and translator, *Love and Conquest: Personal Correspondence of Catherine the Great and Prince Grigory Potemkin* (DeKalb, Illinois: Northern Illinois University Press, 2004), p. 382.

CHAPTER FIVE   PATRON OF THE ARTS

1. W. F. Reddaway, editor, *Documents of Catherine the Great* (*Correspondence with Voltaire and Instructions of 1767*) (Cambridge, England: Cambridge University Press, 1931), p. 42.

2. Voltaire and Catherine the Great, *Voltaire and Catherine the Great: Selected Correspondence*, translated by Anthony Lentin (Cambridge, England: Oriental Research Partners, 1974), p. 167.

Glossary

aesthetic	(es-THEH-tik)—having or showing appreciation of beauty.
annexed	(a-NEKST)—situation in which one country takes over another country or territory.
autocratic	(aw-toe-KRAT-ik)—single ruler governing with unlimited power.
betrothal	(bi-TROH-thul)—engagement; promising to marry.
commerce	(KOM-urss)—the buying and selling of things to make money.
consort	(KON-sort)—the husband or wife or a king or queen.
cosmopolitan	(koz-muh-POL-uh-tuhn)—of or from many parts of the world.
coup	(KOO)—overthrow of an existing government.
dignitaries	(DIG-nih-tare-eez)—people holding high rank or position.
divinity	(di-VIN-ih-tee)—being excellent or very beautiful.
emanating	(EH-meh-nay-ting)—coming out from a source.
fortress	(FOR-triss)—a place that is strengthened against attack.
Kremlin	(KREM-lin)—fortress within the city of Moscow.
memoirs	(MEM-wahrs)—a person writing an account of his or her life.
monarch	(MON-ark)—a ruler with the title of king, queen, emperor, or empress.
orthodox	(OR-thuh-doks)—members of a religion that believe in its older, more traditional teachings.
plague	(PLAYG)—a very serious disease that spreads quickly to many people and often causes death.
provincial	(pruh-VIN-shuhl)—having a limited point of view.
quarries	(KWOR-eez)— places where stone, slate, and similar materials are dug from the ground.
Renaissance	(REH-nuh-sahnss)—period of revival of art and learning in Europe between the fourteenth and sixteenth centuries.
sables	(SAY-buhls)—furs taken from small animals that are similar to weasels.
salvos	(SAL-vohz)—firing guns at the same time.
sovereign	(SAW-vuh-ruhn)—a king or queen; having the highest power.
traversed	(tra-VURSED)—traveled.

For Further Reading

For Young Adults

Brown, Kim Brown. *Russia*. San Diego, California: Greenhaven Press, 1998.

Hatt, Christine. *Catherine the Great*. Milwaukee, Wisconsin: World Almanac Library, 2003.

Meltzer, Milton. *Ten Queens: Portraits of Women in Power*. New York: Dutton, 1998.

Strickler, James E. *Russia of the Tsars*. San Diego, California: Greenhaven Press, 1998.

Works Consulted

Catherine II. *Memoirs of Catherine the Great*. Translated by Katharine Anthony. New York: Tudor Publishing Company, 1935.

Coughlan, Robert. *Elizabeth and Catherine: Empresses of the Russias*. New York: G.P. Putnam, 1974.

Dixon, Simon. *Catherine the Great*. London: Pearson Education Limited, 2001.

LeDonne, John P. *The Russian Empire and the World 1700-1917: The Geopolitics of Expansion and Containment*. New York: Oxford University Press, 1997.

Reddaway, W. F., editor. *Documents of Catherine the Great (Correspondence with Voltaire and Instructions of 1767)*. Cambridge, England: Cambridge University Press, 1931.

Smith, Douglas, editor and translator. *Love and Conquest: Personal Correspondence of Catherine the Great and Prince Grigory Potemkin*. DeKalb, Illinois: Northern Illinois University Press, 2004.

Troyat, Henri. *Catherine the Great*. Translated by Joan Pinkham. New York: E.P. Dutton, 1977.

Voltaire and Catherine the Great. *Voltaire and Catherine the Great: Selected Correspondence*. Translated by Anthony Lentin. Cambridge, England: Oriental Research Partners, 1974.

On the Internet

The Alexander Palace Time Machine
http://www.alexanderpalace.org/palace/catherine

Early Imperial Russia
http://countrystudies.us/russia/4.htm

Hillwood in Focus: The Reign of Catherine the Great
http://www.hillwoodmuseum.org/monthfocus/june.html

Empress Catherine II "the Great" of Russia
http://www.kings.edu/womens_history/catherine

North Park University Chicago: Russian and Eastern Europe Chronology
http://campus.northpark.edu/history/WebChron/EastEurope/CathyGreat

The State Hermitage Museum
http://www.hermitagemuseum.org/

Index